Katie Goes 1

By Catheri

ISBN 978-1477517772

© Copyright Catherine Black 2011

Peru is an exciting country on the Pacific coast of South America, bordered to the north by Ecuador, to the east by Bolivia and to the south by Chile. It is a land of high mountains, jungles, deserts, lost cities and an amazing diversity of people.

The entry point of this trip is Lima the capital of Peru. From Lima the journey takes me by plane to the Inca capital of Cuzco, the jumping off point for Machu Picchu. I take the train to and from Machu Picchu. Then from Cuzco in a south eastern direction to Puno, again by train, a bus ride to the Peruvian Bolivian frontier and another bus to the Bolivian capital La Paz. I want to share this adventure with you.

When to go

I go in September which is spring in the southern hemisphere, and when Lima suffers from the Garua, a grey mist which hangs above Lima like a blanket, blocking out any sun and giving the city a dismal grey look. Perhaps a visit between December and March would in fact be the time to see Lima at its best when the sky is clearer but, like many cities, summer in Lima is hot and humid.

Lima Airport

Lima's airport is small by European standards but functional. On arrival, immigration is dealt with quickly and in an uncomplicated manner. No visa is necessary for Europeans but do check before you go that there have been no changes. Passports must be valid for six months, as is the case when visiting many countries. I am given, free of charge, a tourist card. Please keep this safe as it is required on leaving the country. A few years ago I lost my entry card while in Singapore and later found it hidden with flyers advertising bars, restaurants and hotels. I now have a paper clip at the back of my passport quietly waiting for my next tourist card. So with card securely in place I head out to the arrival terminal. The arrival hall at Jorge Chavez is chaotic. No time wasted waiting for luggage as I only travel with hand luggage. Keep a tight hold on the bag. I won't be bullied into a taxi to be taken to a hotel by a tout. I need to find the desks for Lan Peru to confirm my flights for tomorrow morning. No I don't want a taxi or hotel. It's mad here.

I have bought my flight tickets for Cuzco on-line so I just need to collect them. Ah, on the left hand side of the terminal building are the desks for Lan Peru. I show the security guard my passport and turn left leaving behind the mass of passengers and persistent taxi drivers. The Iberia flight arrived one hour late and now Lan Peru are closing. I am too late to collect the tickets, but they are able to confirm that I am on the morning flight to Cuzco. Just pick up the tickets in the morning.

I have at this point three ways of getting to the hotel in the historic centre of Lima. I can take public transport. I know that bus number 35 or 11 will take me to Plaza 2 de Mayo, but I will need to take a taxi from there to the hotel. Option two I can walk out of the airport terminal to the main road where I can flag down a taxi. These only cost four to seven dollars. Only problem is how safe are they? It is now getting dark. I have heard so many tales of disreputable South American taxi drivers not to be incredibly wary. Option three. For ten dollars I can take an official airport taxi parked outside the Lan Peru desks.

After changing some dollars into Peruvian Sol, I decide on option three. Be sensible. To save five dollars is it worth the risk of being robbed on the way into the city? I step outside to be greeted by a smiling taxi driver wearing a very smart uniform. This part of the airport arrivals is a world apart from the chaos only two hundred meters away.

After double checking the price, me and my small rucksack (which is never put in the boot of a taxi) are installed in the back seat and I am off on the twelve kilometres to the centre. The taxi leaves the lights of the airport, turns into Avenue Elmer Fawcett, the area serving the port and Katie has her first impressions of Lima.

The Centre of Lima

The drive into the city passes many buses which have seen better days but are carrying double the intended number of passengers. Thank goodness I did not take the bus. As I round the dimly lit Plaza 2 de Mayo I begin to wonder if I have not made a dreadful mistake in coming to Peru. Although I know this was and still is the scene of many protests by underfed, badly clothed and poorly housed Peruvians, I am not prepared for such a sad looking place. The only building which does not have what I call the "communist look" is the public showers. We continue for about another three hundred meters and arrive at the Hotel Kamala. I have chosen this hotel because of its close proximity to Jiron de la Union, the pedestrian street which leads to Plaza de Armas.

The taxi stops outside the hotel with its metal portal and guard, and for the second time in half an hour I ask myself "Why have I come here?" But of course I know the answer. Lima is only the gateway to more exciting things.

After arranging for the taxi to pick me up at seven thirty the next morning I go in to see what my "prison" has in store for me. What a pleasant surprise! Nice friendly reception staff, a brightly lit, modern hotel with a distinct Peruvian flavour. For my thirty five dollars I have an enormous room with a sitting area and a dining room with a table for six people. Quite a little apartment. It's a pity I don't know anybody here in Lima to invite for dinner. Just perfect except for the temperature and the musty smell. A quick spruce up and I am ready to hit the town. On this trip showers are not high on my list of to dos as heating is a luxury, and, as I am about to discover, so is hot water.

After getting a map of this part of Lima from the friendly receptionist, the metal bars which cover the entrance door are opened and I am off to explore the city. I know I have to be careful and keep to the well populated streets. With a large unemployed population living in the city, tourists like me are easy pickings. Lima is no different from many other big cities. The possibility of being robbed is real. Keep security in mind but do not let it spoil the fun.

In Peru you are obliged to have identification with you at all times. I have a photocopy of my passport to carry around as I think my passport is safer left in the hotel. It is unlikely I will be asked for identification but being unable to produce this, if stopped by the police, can result in being arrested.

 I turn right along Calle Camana, then right again and I am in Calle Miro Quesada. Can so many people want a pair of glasses? Every shop appears to be an optician's. If you wear glasses bring your prescription with you; the prices are unbelievably cheap. One block and twenty opticians later I arrive at the pedestrian street Jiron de la Union. A quick left turn and my senses are attacked from all angles. The smell of food cooking, the banter of the shop assistants, the chatter of South American Spanish; yes, here I am again in South America. I just love Latin America. Two blocks and I reach the object of this walk, Plaza de Armas, which modern Peru now calls Plaza Mayor. I can visualize in my head every country or city that I want to visit and my picture for Lima is this square at night. All the poverty that exists in Peru is excluded from here. In the centre of the square stands the magnificent seventeenth century bronze fountain. Round the outside of the square are The Cathedral, The Archbishop's Palace, The "Palacio de Gobierno" and the Town Hall. All were renovated in the nineteenth century. It is so romantic. On the benches in the square sit young and not so young couples cuddling. One hour ago I described Lima as dull and grey but from now I will think of Lima as the "cuddly" city.

 Here on the Plaza is the statue of the great Francisco Pizarro who claimed the Inca Empire for the Spanish. The inland capital of Cuzco was of little use to the Spaniards as a capital. They needed a capital on the coast to be able to continue the trade between the new land and the home land. In 1535 Pizarro established Lima as the capital of the

Viceroyship of Peru. The Spanish were to rule Peru until independence in 1824.

I walk on past the elegant statue of Francisco Pizarro on horseback and head for Pasaje Viejo just off the square facing the Cathedral. This small street has a great selection of restaurants. I choose one with a view over the Plaza, select today's special, "chicken-something" at two dollars, sip my glass of Chilean wine and absorb my surroundings.

Off to Cuzco

I never suffer from jetlag, but I am reluctant to stretch out my arm to switch off my dependable travel alarm which is trying to communicate with me. It is six thirty and it is freezing cold. No heating here. There is no way I am showering in this temperature and I wonder how I would survive if I visited The Arctic. I am always amazed by the fact that when I am cold I cannot think. Solution to current situation is of course breakfast. Although it is only six forty five the restaurant is bustly. No buffet here only hot coffee and toast. That will do just nicely.

It is seven twenty-nine and my smiling, uniformed taxi driver and his shining black car are waiting outside. I am returning to Jorge Chávez Airport for my flight to Cuzco. Traffic can be heavy and slow in Lima, so it is best to allow one hour for this trip. My impressions of Lima from the previous evening are confirmed. Even in daylight Lima would not win any competition as a pretty city.

I collect my flight tickets after having agreed that in seven days my taxi driver Carlos will meet me from the LAB flight from La Paz. Nothing lost if he forgets. Now passport control and security. I pass my bag through the scanner. What is in it that is causing a problem? Oh, the heating element for boiling water. They don't know what it is for, so I have to explain that you fill a cup with water put the heating element in the cup, then plug it into the socket and wait for the water to boil and then you can make coffee. The ingenuity of this wonderful apparatus obviously appeals to the girl supervising the scanner because she invites all the workers to come and have a look. She now, with her newly acquired knowledge, explains to them all how this little thing can boil the water for coffee. After a five minute delay during which time the whole workforce of this part of the airport comes to a halt due to my water heater, it is agreed that it is indeed a useful item to have. They are all so enthusiastic about it I am sure that it will be confiscated. Why do I always think the worst when dealing with security personnel? Wrong! Back it goes in my bag.

The departure lounge for internal flights is small. There seems to be some delay in the Cuzco flights. It is simple really. The 10:10 flight will leave one hour later in the slot allocated for the 11.10 flight and the 11.10 flight will leave sometime after that, but nobody knows when. Yes, you've guessed. I am booked on the ten past eleven flight. I could have to wait in a worse place than this. The departure lounge has a superb range of "empanadas" (little meat pies), chocolate cake and other goodies for eating. Oh no! That's a bad sign. Lan Peru are giving out free sandwiches and Inca Cola but no news of the plane. Then sometime around twelve the flight is announced and I am on my way. South American airlines are infamous for chopping flights. I should have reserved the earlier flight or flown Aero Continente which seems to be flying more frequently but Aero Continente did not offer the possibility of online reservation.

The short flight across the Andes is spectacular, as is the landing in Cuzco. The plane just seems to drop in between the mountains. I look out the window as the wing dips and a large grassy green mountain comes up to meet me. The plane rights itself and we swoop down into the valley. I feel like a condor in flight.

Out of the airport and into a taxi. I am now at 3,326 meters above sea level and the air is noticeably thinner. During this trip I will be plagued by altitude sickness. AMS, acute mountain sickness, affects the body due to the lack of oxygen at high altitudes. I have come from Lima which is at sea level up to over three thousand meters so my head is hurting. There is not a lot I can do about it except drink extra liquid and hope that my body makes the necessary adjustments to living at this high altitude. I believe that my body has to make some more red blood cells. After a day or two it should be better.

Five minutes later and I am at Estacion Huancho in Cuzco all prepared for the usual push and shove of railway station ticket windows. I am shown into the ticket office which has tables with two chairs at each down one side, and along the other wall is a long bench. Somebody gives me a ticket with a number on it and I have to sit and wait my turn to be served. No queue jumping here. (Actually I am very familiar with this ticket system as it is the same as used by the butcher in my home town in Spain, except he doesn't have a bench to sit on while you are waiting). It is nearly my turn so I am away to the toilet to retrieve the money from the money belt under my clothes. My turn comes and over I go with reservation printout in hand. I have reserved my tickets by email and now I have to pay for them. I have tickets for tomorrow on the Vista Dome train to Machu Picchu and tickets for the Inca class to Puno for later in the week. These rail journeys are the highlight of this trip and I am going first class. I can't believe how simple it is to reserve tickets from another continent and have them handed to you on arrival. The computer has made travelling so easy to organize.

Then it's out of the station and into another taxi to the centre of

Cuzco, a five minute journey. My hotel here is Plaza de Armas situated on a corner of the square of the same name. As I drive up Avenue Sol, I fall head over heels in love with Cuzco. I think it is like somewhere in South America designed by the Swiss. The sun is shining, the sky is a perfect shade of blue and not a cloud insight but because of the altitude it is cold. I have seen many photographs and read many texts about this town but they are limp in comparison to reality. I really love it here. Daniel the taxi driver agrees to pick me up at five next morning. He is young, a bit rough looking, trying to be with it with his baseball cap back to front, and I think he will never get up at that early time especially as the average taxi fare is only about three dollars. He gives me a big friendly wave as he bumps off on the cobbled road and whirls round the Plaza.

Husband Robert with Plaza de Armas in the back ground.

Perhaps this is a good point to tell you a little about Katie. I am a "travel-holic". I am never happier than when I am visiting new places. I am married to a great guy who has the travel bug nearly as badly as me. Although I write using the first person I am accompanied on all my travels by husband Robert.

Pushing open the door of Hostal Plaza de Armas, I have the feeling that my "nose" for finding good, small, reasonably priced hotels has worked again. Choosing hotels from information you have is like buying wine. If you buy an expensive bottle, it is normally good but the expert is the person who can choose a good bottle of cheap plonk.

At reception I am offered a quiet interior room or a room with a view and noise. I open the window of my first floor room. The views down Ave. Sol and of the Plaza to my left take my breath away (or is it the stairs and altitude). Price for quality this little hostel is scoring high. Heated room, hot water, modern bathroom, TV, excellent position and only fifty-four dollars a night. Due to the number of visitors, Cuzco has no shortage of good hotels but the more expensive e.g. Hotel Don Carlos, Royal Inca I and ll, and Pasada Del Inca lose out on being further from the centre. All of Cuzco radiates out from the Plaza de Armas, and I want to stay here.

Hostal Plaza de Armas Cuzco

I am a person of the present and history is not my favourite subject but here in the oldest continuously inhabited city in the continent of South America you cannot escape being touched by its past. Cuzco is a unique city with an age old culture. Names like Manco Capac, Inca Roca and Pachacutec. Who were they? They have such a magical sound. Every school child learns about the Incas. Wouldn't it be great if a visit here to Cuzco, the ancient capital of the Inca Empire, was part of the school curriculum.

My husband sitting on the balcony in Café Bagdad with the Plaza de Armas and the Andes in the background

A walk round the Plaza tells me I won't have any problem finding dinner tonight. Three sides of the outer perimeter are just cafés and restaurants, some with rather precariously looking balconies overhanging the street. The cold is beginning to penetrate my bones so it's time to try some of Cuzco's famous mulled wine or perhaps even a "mate de coca" (coca tea). Sitting in Café Bagdad (a very South American name), where I am lucky enough to have one of the four tables on the balcony, I have time to reflect on this wonderful city. It is a small city but seems more like a big market town. Below me, on the square, the Quechua speaking indigenous people, in their colourful clothes, go about their day as if in a different world from mine. I watch the Peruvian women with their jet black pleated hair and cushion cover hats chatting away in a language I will never understand. On their backs they have the traditional colourful striped red and blue blanket, carrying anything from firewood to a baby. Behind the two storey buildings, with their red tiled roofs, only the tower of San Francisco church protrudes and behind this the Andes.

This is the Third World with its poverty and lack of hygiene but here there is something magical. The influx of visitors has brought modern hotels, restaurants as good as in the city, modern cars but at the same time the descendants of the mighty Incas have retained their Quechua language and the city very much belongs to them. I am only a visitor for two days and I feel privileged to be here.

As the sun disappears the skyline is broken by the wisps of smoke from the wood burning stoves and the whole town smells of burning wood.

I leave the warmth of Café Bagdad, walk past the famous cathedral and turn left up Calle Triunfo. The shops are full of brightly coloured woven goods, bags, hats, table mats and purses. No problem finding a present or souvenir here and they are so light to carry. Oh look at these adorable Peruvian hats with the flaps that cover the ears. I cross the square again heading for more retail therapy in the pedestrian streets of Suecia and Procuradores. In front of the Cathedral I am invited to have my photo taken with a group of women. Why not? It will look good in the photo album. Even in these days of digital photos I like to make prints of photos taken and make an album of photos and mementos of my trip. There is nothing better than to spend a wet Sunday looking at the photo album and reliving the experience.

Here is the photo taken on the steps outside the Cathedral in Cuzco. (I am the one in the white cardigan)

Dinner time. Now which of these restaurants is going to have the pleasure of my company? I am looking for somewhere a little up-market but not too expensive. I am a little choosy about where I eat. Knowing that Cuzco has more dangerous, daring thieves than even Lima, I am eating somewhere on the well lit Plaza.

Walking around looking at menus and restaurants is not proving to be as easy as I expected. It would appear that every restaurant wants me. I walk a few steps and three dozen menus, from three dozen different restaurants, each one claiming to be the best in town, are thrust into my hand. I try to read the one which is uppermost but by the time I get to the main courses this menu is well down the bundle in my hand, with the new arrivals placing their menus on top. I realize that reading the menu as a way of choosing an eating place is just not going to work. I have another idea. I cross into the middle of Plaza de Armas, stand next to the fountain, out of reach of any menu, and look round at the restaurants from a safe distance. The Pachacutec Grill Bar on the corner at Portal de Panes catches my eye. Pachacutec? Who is he again? Confident with my decision I cross the road again to be met by the army of menu carriers. Don't look left or right. Straight in I go. Must have good long vision. The restaurant is very nice. On the wall is a magnificent painting of a warrior sitting on a throne. On his head are beautiful brown and red feathers. He is definitely somebody important. Of course, he is none other than Pachacutec. After spending the afternoon here I know a little about this Inca. He was the one who saved Cuzco from its tribal enemies the Chancas. When the chips were down during a battle his father and brother Urco accepted defeat and fled, but Pachacutec rallied the troops and defeated the Chancas. During his reign Cuzco grew from a hamlet into an empire and some believe that Machu Picchu was built as an estate for him. Many of the famous buildings built around Cuzco, the sun temple of Coricancha and the fortress of Sacayhuaman were constructed during his reign. I believe that in modern Peru he is still regarded as a hero.

And here am I, sitting within the stone walls of the former palace of the great Inca Pachacutec, about to order dinner. Spicy pork, pork ribs, kebab or what about roast guinea pig? Don't think so. My children, especially my daughter, would never forgive me. The dinner is excellent. I am sure Pachacutec would agree. Courtesy of the restaurant we have our Pisco Sour. The first and last for me when I find out that it has raw egg whites in the recipe.

This has been an action packed day. Flying from Lima to Cuzco, the capital of the Inca Empire. Exploring the streets with their massive Inca built stone walls, seeing the Quechua speaking descendants of the

Incas, learning a little about the Incas; what an incredible experience this has been.

I lie in bed unable to sleep. At this altitude when your head hits the pillow, it is as if the pillow is made of concrete. I think about the wonderful place modern day Cuzco is, and the changes here since Hiram Bingham found Machu Picchu in 1911. I try to imagine the city as it was when Francisco Pizarro (remember the statue in Lima) came looting. Whether it was the British in Burma, the Spanish in South America or the French in South East Asia the story is the same. They looted and destroyed both the civilization and culture.

Machu Picchu

It is four thirty and I have to get up. What did I eat last night that did not like me? After various visits to the toilet I try breakfast. Oh forget it, which is a shame as the Hostal Plaza de Armas has a very nice breakfast room overlooking the square. Am I suffering from altitude sickness or a good old fashioned tummy bug? The phone rings and I am informed that my taxi is waiting. Wrong again. Daniel is up at the crack of dawn to earn three dollars. I drag myself downstairs and flop into the waiting taxi. This is my big day. I have flown thirteen hours from Madrid to Lima, then flown another hour to Cuzco. Why? To go by train to Machu Picchu and I am feeling lousy.

Why do all taxi drivers feel it is their duty to educate me? Even at this early hour I am subjected to a history lesson. Five minutes and one history class later I arrive at San Pedro Station. Cuzco has two stations. This station, San Pedro, principally serves only Machu Picchu. The area round this station is not too good. Nearby is the Mercado Central and the area is known for its pickpockets and bag snatchers. I enter the station and once my ticket is checked I am shown onto the train. How did they know? I have a seat fairly near the toilet. The train is freezing cold. At exactly six the train is off on its hundred kilometre journey.

I pass adobe houses two storeys high. Some are colourfully painted. Two thirds of the houses in rural areas in Peru are made from adobe. They are called the poor man's death trap. Peru is prone to earthquakes and during an earth quake these houses, which are made from bricks of sun dried mud and straw, just collapse outwards. The tiled roof, weighing about ten tons, falls in and crushes the occupants. I read an article recently that it is fairly easy to strengthen the walls with bamboo or eucalyptus poles and this structural change allows the walls and the roof to absorb the vibrations of an earthquake. I hope that the ones I am looking at have been built using bamboo.

This train journey out of Cuzco is a rail traveller's delight. It is a switchback. The track out from Cuzco is so steep that the train has to shunt backwards and forwards four or five times to change levels. This is fascinating and quite a feat of engineering. During the half hour that this takes, the view of Cuzco below is incredible. I love travelling by train. For me it is the best way of getting around. You meet local people and see the countryside. This train however is a little different. There are no local people on it as it is the "Vista Dome" a special train for tourists. The roof and the sides are of glass so you can see everything. Local people on this route use the third class train which is obviously much cheaper. Some backpackers on a budget also use this train but it is not recommended because of the number of thefts. When the train goes into a tunnel your backpack goes AWOL.

The first stop is in Poroy, three thousand six hundred and seventy three meters above sea-level. This is the highest point on this line. The train then zigzags as it descends to The Sacred Valley of the Incas. Peru Rail take tourism seriously and the train is spotlessly clean and very comfortable. One hour out of Cuzco and breakfast is served. For me no thank you but could you please put some heat through the train? One hour into the journey and the temperature is still low. I am not feeling very well and I don't like feeling this way. I am super careful what I eat and drink. On trips like this I never eat salad or uncooked food and I clean my teeth with bottled water.

The "Vista Dome" carriage is fantastic. As we enter the gulleys and gorges I can see up the two sides. We pass mountain streams and small hamlets where people live in a way not too different from their Inca ancestors, cultivating maize and potatoes and looking after llamas. In one part of the journey the railway line hugs the side of the Andes Mountains and you feel so close to these monsters. I don't know the names of all the peaks I am passing. Some people in the coach obviously find it important to do so and have a local guide on the train with them explaining where they are and telling them what to look at. Personally I find them an intrusion in my airspace; they never stop talking. I just want to look at everything and let it all seep in. The web site of Peru Rail, where you can now buy tickets online, also has good information on what you can see en route. At Km 88 the train stops for the energetic to alight. Here they begin their three or four day hike on the Inca Trail. I watch them struggle off the train with enormous backpacks. I can't imagine any fun in trailing around with all that luggage. Even when I was much younger it would not have had any appeal for me. Perhaps I am just a little jealous of these young fit people.

The train approaches the town of Aguas Calientes and I am feeling much better. As I am in a Spanish speaking country I think "Gracias a Dios". The scenery on this journey has been so spectacular I haven't had time to think about my personal state. The train draws to a halt in Aguas Calientes and the adrenalin is flowing fast. Sometimes I am so complacent about where I am and what I am seeing and other times I can't believe that it is real. As I step from the train on to the platform big tears of happiness roll down my cheek.

For the last five years I have wanted to come here. Why has it taken me so long?

First of all, the price. This is an expensive trip taking into account the cost of return tickets from Europe to Lima, a flight from Lima to Cuzco and a flight from La Paz back to Lima. Three flights, plus two train journeys in first class. So why have I managed it now? I was lucky enough to get a very good price, special offer with Iberia the Spanish airline. Too good to miss! My second reason for delaying is that I am terrified of twisting mountain roads and thirdly in my younger days Peru was plagued by problems caused by the Maoist terrorist group Sendero Luminoso, who campaigned against the government from 1980 until the early 1990s. The good price for the flights helped me overcome my fears and now I'm really glad I have come.

I know I have to go down the steps from the station and along the old railway line. So off I go with the masses towards the waiting buses. This can't be described as an adventure because there are so many tourists. I think I am so special to be here but there are a lot of other lucky people here too. The old railway line is lined with restaurants and stalls selling souvenirs. I promise to have a look on the way back. On the right hand side a few meters down the track is a booth selling tickets for the buses which run up and down to Machu Picchu. Many people walk on past this. This explains the number of guides on the train. In Lima and Cuzco they sell a package which includes the return train fare, a guide, the bus connection, entrance to Machu Picchu with lunch at hotel Machu Picchu. I think that doing this trip, buying tickets as I go, will save me half the price of the package. I will not have a guide but I am not too keen on guides. If you do your homework about the place you are visiting you should know what there is to see before you go. Then there's lunch. With so many eating places on the old railway line it shouldn't be a problem. With the ticket for the bus bought, I join the short queue for the bus. I content myself that it looks relatively modern and I assume that the brakes are fine. I could ask the driver to do an emergency stop just to reassure me but I don't think he would. This is what I have dreaded. A corkscrew road. Do you want to see Machu Picchu I ask myself? If so, just get on the bus; sit down shut your eyes. It only takes ten minutes. The bus leaves Aguas Calientes and crosses the bridge. On both sides are towering mountains heavily forested. Up and up I go. We leave the tarred road behind and continue up a dirt track. Ha ha! I look at a girl sitting near me. No, she hasn't got her eyes closed, has she?

I am happy to be off the bus but in reality the trip up was not as bad as I had imagined. I pay the twenty dollar entrance fee at the guarded ticket gate and walk along the footpath for about a hundred meters. My head is feeling slightly dizzy and the butterflies in my stomach are fluttering about. And there it is! The picture I have seen so many times in magazines like National Geographic is there in front of me, but it isn't a picture, it is the real thing. I stand there staring, fighting back the tears of emotion. Although over the years I have become a world traveller, I still feel so lucky to be able to witness the wonders of the world I live in. Machu Picchu, the lost city of the Incas, and I am finally here. I can begin to understand how Hiram Bingham must have felt when he discovered it in 1911.

Where should I start exploring. It doesn't really matter which order I look at things. I see on the map names like the Royal Tomb, the Sacred Plaza, the House of the High Priest, the Temple of the Three Windows but not being into archaeology in a big way, I find it difficult to know if it had been a temple or a tomb. The greatest thing is the sheer height of the mountains and I feel as if I am standing on top of the world. The day is clear and I have a perfect view.

On the eastern slopes of the Andes, in the middle of a tropical forest, I wander for hours looking at the polished stones, the terraced landscape and the "alpacas". These wonderful, sociable animals communicating with each other with humming noises and head movements. They look so cuddly and soft. They are not very big, weighing between one hundred and one hundred and eighty pounds. It is interesting to learn that the female has a single birth. It is very rare for an alpaca to give birth to twins. At first glance they appear to be white, brown, grey and black in colour but actually they can have twenty two natural colours. I could sit here all day just watching them graze. I wonder do they realize that they have such a famous address.

This mountain air is making me peckish. I know that eating in here is frowned upon. I do not want one of the many guards blowing his whistle at me because I am eating my crisps and Babybel cheese. Like a naughty school child I opt for putting a few discreet handfuls of potato crisps from my rucksack into my mouth. Don't take the crisp bag out of the rucksack. A coffee shop would be a welcome sight but I think it would look out of place.

Two hours later, and a camera full of photographs, I have absorbed all the wonder. It never ceases to amaze me that I can travel for days to reach what I crave to see and after a short time I have seen everything.

Oh dear. The bus again. The bus back down is better because every curve is one less to go but now we have buses making their way up while we are going down. I think that the road is not wide enough for our bus but miraculously two buses can pass. Back in Aguas Calientes I am not sure which has impressed me most, the Lost City of the Incas or the sheer height of the mountains. This time as I walk back along the old railway track, through the stalls of souvenirs, I take time to look at the pretty jewellery made from local stones. I select a necklace of pale blue stones as my memento of the day.

As it is only one o'clock and my train doesn't leave till three I am going to explore Aguas Calientes. I walk through this charming town and I wish I could spend more time here. I normally prefer beaches, jungles and deserts to mountains but here is different. The proximity of these monsters is fantastic. I would like to spend the night here in the middle of the mountains. I always think that from Cuzco to Machu Picchu you go up when I know in reality you go down. Machu Picchu stands at a height of two thousand four hundred and thirty metres above sea-level which is nearly nine hundred meters in altitude less than Cuzco thus making it easier to breathe here. From Machu Picchu there is a path which snakes its way down to Aguas Calientes. That would be good to do if I was younger and fitter but a four hour walk would be too ambitious for me. Finding lunch is easy as there are a number of restaurants in the town. I choose one near the Plaza.

One thing which did strike me at Machu Picchu was the number of people my age and over, doing the visit with a guide and group. At first you think that this takes a lot of the hassle out of the trip having someone to take care of you. In actual fact it is the opposite. I felt so sorry for one mature couple I saw who were with a group. The guide was way out in front with the majority of the tourists behind her and two sixty year olds lagging well behind. It was obvious that their main objective was to keep up with the group rather than enjoying their surroundings. To have come so far and be marched round so fast was a crime. The terrain round Machu Picchu is slightly difficult but when you are setting your own pace it's not too bad. Further on I met three young people in their twenties. One of the three had badly deformed legs and had to use crutches. She, unlike the older couple, was thoroughly enjoying herself getting along at her own pace. At one point where the steps were proving a little difficult for her, she handed the crutches to one of the friends and continued the trip bouncing up the steps on her bottom. Well done you!

Lunch over and it's time for the train back to Cuzco. It is a pity that darkness falls so soon and the unforgettable views from the window disappear to remain only in my mind. The zigzag shunting of the train just before Cuzco is twice as impressive in the dark. The view from above of the floodlit church and cathedral on the Plaza de Armas is spectacular.

The push and shove of taxi drivers as I exit San Pedro railway station is reminiscent of the airport in Lima. They are so keen on getting a fare that they almost make it impossible to get out. What part of "no" do they not understand? I get quite angry when I am hassled like this. If I want a taxi, I want a taxi, but shouting louder at me will not change my mind. I look behind the angry mob of taxi drivers and Daniel is standing waiting across the road. I push my way through and cross the street and jump into his taxi. As I open the door I nearly choke on the air freshener he has sprayed inside. He is really trying to impress me. Perhaps I should tell him I was impressed when he arrived at the crack of dawn this morning. Was it only this morning I left Cuzco? It has been a long wonderful day.

My objective for dinner is to run the gauntlet of the menu carriers. I now know the trick. Decide where to go before leaving the hotel. I will of course try another on the Plaza de Armas.

The Road to Puno

Today I am off on my second train journey. Daniel is once again at the hotel five minutes early. I have to say that this young lad will be one of the good memories of this trip. His service as a taxi driver has taken a lot of the pressure of me. His attempts to teach me some of the Quechua language have been unsuccessful but what do you expect in ten minute trips. I also have to admit that I am not as fond of the folk music of the area as he is. I arrive at Estacion Huancho, where I first met Daniel, in good time for the train to Puno. We say our goodbyes and off he goes wearing his back-to-front baseball cap.

The train leaves punctually at eight o'clock. This is what I call a classy train. I believe it was in service in Asia before being bought by Peru Rail. The outside is beautifully painted blue and gold. The interior is like the Orient Express. Down the right hand side are tables for two just like in a restaurant and on the left hand side tables for four. No ordinary train seats here. They are comfy armchairs. As I look around I wish that my dad could see this. He worked for British Rail and gave me my love of trains, but he has never been in a train like this. He was the guard on the train on one of the Queen's visits to Scotland and I doubt if the train was better than this.

Breakfast is served as the train heads south east on the first part of this ten hour journey. This journey has been described as one of the best rail journeys in the world. It follows the Huatanay River through green fields passing the village of Oropesa twenty-five kilometres from Cuzco. This village is worth a mention as it has forty-seven bakeries which supply Cuzco with bread. At kilometre 186 the Cuzco hills are left behind as the train enters the high plains or Altiplano and continues its climb to La Raya, the highest point of the journey. A three course lunch is served. The food and service are excellent. I love avocados and in Peru they seem to be part of every dish.

Just after lunch the train stops at La Raya. I am now at four thousand, three hundred and twenty-one metres above sea level. The train door is opened. I move to go out when the air (or should I say the lack of air) smacks me on the face. I can hardly draw a breath. I stand on the top step of the train holding onto the railing for a few minutes. Oh look! It's a market. The local people have brought their wares to sell. On the left of the train are mountains and to the right are all these colourful people who have set up their stalls only for this train stop. I suppose if you live in such a remote place you don't see much passing trade. The stall I go to look at is manned by three generations of the same family. The two older women and a girl about seven years old are dressed the same. Perched on their heads are bright red sombrero styled hats. I know that this is the style but they look too small for them. Actually at this temperature a good woolly bonnet would be more appropriate. They are all wearing black skirts which are beautifully trimmed with bright coloured braiding and the mother and child have waistcoats to match.

Now let's look at what's on sale. Jerseys all sizes in natural browns, fawn and cream colours. These have been made with wool from alpacas, llamas and vicunas. They are beautifully made. Look over here and they have little animals made from fur. What else for sale? The multicoloured blankets. I could buy one in case my bag bursts, put all my things in it, sling it on my back and go native. On the ground near the stalls are the same blankets containing extra stock if the need should arise. I find that these people are not too interested in selling. It seems strange to have gone to so much work and not be a little more aggressive in trying to sell. Silly me, it is easier to stand and have your photograph taken for a few Sol, than spend hours knitting in bad light damaging your eyes in the process. Who can blame them? Life at this altitude in such a remote place must be hard and some photos from here are a must for the photograph album. After ten minutes, there are two loud blasts from the train's horn informing everybody that the shopping trip is over and it's time to roll. The train is still two hundred kilometres from Juliaca.

Back on the train I sit and think about the difference in lifestyle between these people and the people of Europe. Where do I start? I take so much for granted. No flushing toilet! Unimaginable. No washing machine, no microwave. How could I get by? Are they happy? Am I happy? Too much psychology. One positive thing about travelling is that it makes you think about other people and teaches you to appreciate what you have.

At the end of the train the last coach is the observation coach. I think it is time to explore the train. As I make my way to the rear, I see a woman who is not enjoying the trip as much as me. She is being attended by two Peru rail staff. She is connected to the oxygen supply which is carried on this train. At this altitude AMS is a real problem. I have a mild sore head and am a little breathless. I admit that I am a little concerned about AMS but hope my body can adapt. I pacify myself by saying that for some reason older people are not so affected and the only practical thing I can do is to keep drinking water and no alcohol. I know I should have spent more time in Cuzco to acclimatise but it is too late now.

Katie enjoys the crisp air

The observation coach has large windows down both sides and on the roof, giving great panoramic views of the mountains. Down the centre are two rows of continuous seats facing the windows. The train continues through kilometre after kilometre of flat arid land and small farms with grazing alpaca and their big cousins, the llama. I read that in Puno I will find llama on the menu. The alpacas are luckier as they are kept mainly as a source of wool. Alpaca wool is very fine and makes great cloth. At the very end of the train the carriage is open allowing me to have a great view. I can spend hours looking out of train windows almost neurotic that I will miss seeing something. Oh this is great and not too cold and, even better, there is nobody else here. I am not an unsociable person but sometimes it is good not to have to make conversation as is the case here. It would be an intrusion.

"The Market Place"

We approach a bigger town where the market occupies both sides of the railway line and the track too. There is an enormous amount of scuffling around as pots, plastic basins and other house hold goods are removed from the track to let the train pass. The moment the train passes everything is moved back onto the track and it is back to business. For me, the incredible thing about this is the speed at which everything is moved from and back onto the track. One thing for sure is that this is not a boring train journey.

We are now approaching Juliaca which means that I am only about an hour and a half from Puno. The train makes its way through the streets cutting the town in half. At the side of the line mechanics are repairing old vehicles, people are wandering everywhere. I am glad I am not getting off here; it is not a pretty town. Apparently Juliaca railway station has a welcoming party of thieves to greet arriving passengers. Juliaca has a population of over one hundred thousand and is the biggest town in the region. A short stop here and I am now on the last section of the trip and I should be seeing Lake Titicaca soon, the highest lake in the world. TITICACA! What a magical sounding name! About fifty kilometres later I get my first glimpse. As the train approaches Puno it goes through some very marshy land, with Totora reeds and "sea" weed, and draws to a halt ten wonderful hours after leaving Cuzco. Ten hours and on time!

I am staying at Hospedaje Pukara and as agreed they have a pick up meeting the train. I don't appear to be the only traveller who has chosen this little hostal. I make my way across to the van and see that my travelling companion is the woman who was having the oxygen on the train. I am glad to see that she is better. The hotel from the station is only half a kilometre but at this altitude with luggage that is quite a walk as I am still at over three thousand, eight hundred metres above sea level. I enter the hotel and admire the floor-to-ceiling mural in the reception. It was to be the only thing I "admired" about this hostal. In the information about this hotel it claimed to have heating. In the room is an oil filled radiator, the cable of which has bare wires, a real fire hazard. The bed has clean sheets but on top are three grubby blankets. The walls are dirty with even boot prints. I am always boasting about my ability to choose a good medium priced hotel but this time I have failed. I ask at reception if they have another room. On inspection it has the same qualities as the one I am in. Just accept that I botched this up. A walk through the town tells me that it is fairly ordinary. If it wasn't for the floating islands I would not stay.

Puno does have about a dozen presentable eating places. Now for dinner. I order a pizza which I play with. I am not hungry and my head hurts. I am definitely being affected by altitude sickness. I go back to my hostal, wishing I had chosen Hotel Colon Inn or even the new hotel on the lake with oxygen pumped into the bedrooms. From the information I had, I thought that Colon Inn was further from the hub of things but it is only round the corner from where I am. My head hits the pillow, another one filled with concrete.

Lake Titicaca

I am up bright and early having had a restless night. I climb the narrow stairs to the covered roof for breakfast. It is not....well let's just say it is not in the same league as yesterday's breakfast on the train. OK, I am not here in Peru to do a Master Chef programme on breakfasts. Today I am going to visit the Floating Islands and the Uro people. I think I can walk to the port. I saw it from the roof top while having "breakfast".

Out of the hotel and straight on. Yes, I'm right. The distance to the lakeshore is very walkable. I arrive at the small jetty, wait for a few minutes and then I am off in a motor boat crossing Lake Titicaca. I notice that my head only hurts when I am not doing something exciting. This morning it is fine.

The motor boat crosses a perfectly calm lake and if you didn't know that the floating islands existed, you would enjoy the boat trip on the lake on its own merit. I arrive about twenty minutes later at one of the floating islands. In Inca times there were about forty of these islands protected in the Bay of Puno. It is said that the Uros made their homes here to escape the fighting on the main land.

I can't believe this. As I step on to the island it moves. It is completely made of layer upon layer of the totora reeds that grow in the lake. There are square houses and round houses all made from reeds. There is a school for the younger children and it is made from reeds. The older ones have to go to school in Puno. I notice that there are no teenagers about. There is a post office too. It is a proper island community except that the islands and the buildings are all made from reeds. As the reeds on the bottom begin to rot new reeds are placed on top.

Here we see "free range" guinea-pigs which provide the main source of meat. The women bake bread in stone ovens and cook on fires built on layers of stones to protect the reeds.

The children play happily on their reed toys and the men go fishing in their boats made of reeds. I notice that each reed boat has an animal face. Would I like a tour of some other islands on a reed boat? Of course! In I get with husband and some other tourists. I hope that this canoe is water tight. It is incredible all these islands and not a building made of anything but reeds. Some islands are big while some are small. At one time a newly married couple would build their own island and live there but now the people live in communities on bigger islands.

As we head back to the island from where we started, the boat man hands me a tin. I soon realize I have to pass this round to collect payment for the experience. Fair enough, but why did he give me the job? Kot-suna or the people of the lake as they call themselves believe that the lake belongs to them and as well as fishing, tourism is their main source of income. It is not possible to visit all the islands as some do not allow access to tourists. They are only for living on.

This really is a remarkable country. Yesterday I was in contact with people who live in remote mountain regions, the day before that with people who are the ancestors of the Incas, and today people who live their life totally on water.

Back on the motor boat to Puno and I have time to admire Lake Titicaca, this one hundred and seventy kilometre long stretch of water which separates Peru and Bolivia. At three thousand, eight hundred and twenty meters above sea level it is the highest navigable lake in the world. It is also South America's largest lake and the world's largest lake over two thousand meters. The air is crystal clear and the sky and the lake a deep blue.

Back on dry land and time to explore Puno. First, a cup of coffee to heat me up. Puno has a selection of coffee bars so it is not too difficult. In day light hours this little town is nicer than I thought yesterday. Perhaps I was unkind to the town when in fact it was the hostal I didn't like. There is still nothing of interest here to keep me another day so tomorrow I am off to cross the frontier and into Bolivia.

Lying in bed in my less than salubrious room I reflect on what I have seen today. For me seeing the floating islands was incredible. They are unique. Where else in the world do you have a community of people who live like that?

But the problems these people must face are enormous. Can you imagine living in a small hut with a floor of reeds which is probably damp? Imagine the bed also made of reeds. All the family living in the same hut and sleeping in one bed. The women wear layers of clothing to protect them from the cold, but can you imagine trying to get into these on a cold damp morning? The men leave the islands to sell their fish on the mainland but the women seldom leave the island. The cooking is perhaps one of the easiest chores. What about looking after the children? That must be a nightmare. How can you let a two or three year old have any freedom when you are living on a moving island surrounded by freezing water. When I think about the practicalities of living such a life style my exhilaration fades a little.

Off to Bolivia

It is eight o'clock in the morning and I am all ready to take the bus to the Bolivian frontier at Yunguyo. I have a bus ticket with a company called Colectur. They send a minivan to the hotel which takes me to the bus station in Puno. I am soon on the two and a half hour drive round Lake Titicaca. I read in the tourist information that the lake is also called Puma Gris and Puma de Piedra. The first part of the bus journey has nice views of the shimmering lake as we drive south. Eighteen kilometres from Puno I drive through the little town of Chucuito with its pretty church. Here we leave the lakeside behind and turn inland to Acora then Llave. From Llave it is a thirty kilometre drive to Juli where we are once again following the shoreline of Lake Titicaca. From Juli another thirty kilometres following the lakeside brings me to Pomata, one hundred and six kilometres from Puno and then on to the frontier at Yunguyo.

When I bought the bus ticket for La Paz in Bolivia the girl in Puno explained that the bus from Puno only goes to a lake side town in Bolivia called Copacabana. In Copacabana I have to change buses to continue to La Paz. It is a direct service with a change of bus.

The bus is now approaching the frontier and what a fiesta. Each side of the street is a mass of stalls selling everything imaginable. Oh, look at these solid wooden beds. This is an amazing sight. As I look out of the bus window I see all these bowler-hatted women in the foreground, with their bundles wrapped in striped blankets and strapped to their backs, and in the background the blue of Lake Titicaca.

All the passengers have to get off the bus and walk through the market to the frontier post, get stamped out of Peru, walk on a little and get stamped into Bolivia. The border formalities are quick and the bus is soon on its way. I have just left Peru and am now on my way to La Paz the capital of Bolivia, or am I?

Accompanying the bus is a representative of the bus company. I noticed him at the frontier in deep conversation with another man who had a worried expression on his face. As the bus picks up speed on its way to Copacabana the representative stands up at the front of the bus, clears his throat and announces that the bus from La Paz will not meet this bus as is normal, because there is a strike in Bolivia. It appears all the passengers will be abandoned in Copacabana. That is exactly what happened. The bus stopped in Copacabana. Everybody got off except the representative who promised that at noon tomorrow the bus coming from La Paz would pick us all up and continue the journey. I stand in the square in Copacabana and watch the bus turn and head back for Peru. Should I do that too?

Return to Lima

I did eventually get to Bolivia and now I am back in Lima airport. I am walking towards immigration when I hear a female voice shout out, "there's the woman with the utensil for making cappuccino". Wow I am famous here in Lima. How did she recognize me? I suppose in a country where everybody has jet black hair a blonde is not too difficult to spot.

My son always laughs at me saying that only a Scottish person could be so mean as to make coffee in a hotel room rather than go to a bar or order room service. This is not the case. It is purely for convenience. I sometimes wake up early, sometimes with the difference of time zones, and do not want to go looking for a coffee shop but want a coffee. So I take a coffee making kit with me. I have also lived enough time in mainland Europe to know the difference between good coffee and coffee served for example in the USA. Anyway I do not need to defend my need for a decent cup of coffee, where and when I want it. Up-market hotels acknowledge this requirement and supply tea and coffee making equipment in their rooms, but I don't always stay in this class of hotel.

It is a good feeling when you are in a foreign country but know exactly where you are, and are familiar with things, because you have been before. With my previously acquired knowledge I avoid all the hassle at arrivals and go directly to the exit opposite Lan Peru offices. Sure enough, there is taxi driver Carlos patiently waiting. This time in Lima I am staying, not in the city centre, but in the up market suburb of Miraflores. It is a little further to Miraflores from the airport than the city centre and the taxi costs me sixteen dollars which I think is a little high, but I suppose the taxi driver thinks that if you can afford a hotel in Miraflores you can afford a couple of extra dollars for the taxi. Perhaps he is right and, after all, he was waiting for me. When I was younger I would stand and haggle over a dollar if I thought I was being overcharged, but now I don't. It only causes friction between me and my travelling companion, my husband.

The taxi stops outside El Pardo Hilton hotel. It is quite different from the first hotel I had in this city. It stands twelve storeys high with a roof top swimming pool and has no metal shutter over the principal door. The bellboy arrives with the luggage trolley and looks very surprised as I walk past him with my small rucksack on my back. No, I haven't got a suitcase.

This hotel is my base for three nights. This is too much time to spend here but I planned a buffer of a few days so I would get back from Bolivia in time to catch the longhaul flight back to Europe. On this occasion I have been proved right. The problem was not only in getting to Bolivia but also getting out of it. I was lucky. The day after I left, the airport at La Paz was closed because of the internal strife. I just got out in time and now I have three days in a modern hotel with all the facilities to relax.

Time for a look around Miraflores. What do I know about Miraflores? It is eight kilometres south from downtown Lima and is on the Pacific Coast. It has many beaches, which are popular with the people from Lima, the biggest being Playa Costa Verde. I believe on Sundays in the summer months it is too popular to be nice. Miraflores is Lima's up market residential area with good hotels, restaurants and entertainment.

Out of the hotel and turn left along Avenue José Pardo to the Ovalo, a roundabout. Here I turn right and go towards the coast passing Parque Central and Parque Kennedy. It is a pleasant walk but not very exciting. One thing I am enjoying is to be able to leave my money and important things behind, locked in the safe in my room. I think that it is often a good investment to choose a hotel, even if it is a little more expensive, if it has a safe deposit box in the room.

I continue walking for over a kilometre and am rewarded with a view of the Pacific Ocean. The beach is not particularly nice but that is my opinion of many beaches. I am lucky to live in a town in Spain which has a wonderful beach, so to impress me the beach has got to be good. Perhaps it looks better in summer than on this dull spring day. It is also not easy to reach. From the Circuito de Playas, the coastal road, it is a substantial downward climb to the stony beach.

By the time I arrive back at the hotel I have walked about four kilometres. From the hub of Miraflores to the beach is about a kilometre. As a holiday resort I would give this a very low score. It is a much safer place to be than the centre of Lima but I know which I prefer.

Back at the hotel and it is time for a swim. Up twelve floors I go to the rooftop indoor pool. The views are very nice but the pool and surrounding area are very cold. No swimming. Again perhaps it is better in the summer.

Finding dinner here in Miraflores is easy. In the hotel there is a nice looking restaurant but I think I will try somewhere out on the town.

Should I go back down to Diagonal nicknamed "Pizza Street" for some Italian food? This is the street I walked down to the coast and I did see many nice eating places. Sometimes I wonder what we ate before pasta and pizza hit the international trail. It doesn't matter which city in the world you are in you can always eat a pizza. If you don't speak the language and the menu is not translated it is often a safe bet. In some parts of Japan I have to confess that I ate Indian food because the menus were only in Japanese, but in an Indian restaurant in Japan I could recognise the names of the curries.

On this trip language is not a problem. I speak enough Spanish to order what I want. I actually find that the Spanish spoken here in Peru is very easy to understand. So let's find a Peruvian restaurant. Given that I am in Peru that shouldn't be too difficult. Eating in Peru has been a sheer delight for me. The restaurants are clean, the service good, the food tasty and the final bill very palatable. I have read that Las Tejas in Diez Canseco Street has good Peruvian food. Diez Canseco is just on a bit from the church of la Virgin Milagrosa. I know where that is. I often find that choosing somewhere to go heads me in a certain direction in a positive manner even if I find somewhere different en route or diverge and head off in the completely opposite direction. There is nothing worse than not knowing where to go.

Last Day

Miraflores might have the top-end restaurants, top grade hotels, shopping malls and leafy streets but I am getting bored so I am off using public transport to the centre of Lima to explore more. Back to the "Ovalo" and look for a bus going up Avenue Arequipa. I don't have long to wait when a rusty old bus full of people stops for me. The people move up the bus and I get on. As we continue towards the centre we have to move up the bus as even more passengers squeeze on. Buses like this are fun. You are travelling with the local people, experiencing the city life like they are. It is easier to go "native" when staying in a good hotel where it is safer to leave your belongings behind. I only have enough money on me for a basic lunch, buying some things I see and the taxi fare back to the hotel. My passport and credit cards are left behind in the hotel safe. I get off the bus in the centre near the Sheraton Hotel Lima. I wander round Parque Italiano then north up Jiron Belen to Plaza San Martin and finally I am back in Jiron de la Union, the pedestrian street where I had so much fun on the first evening in Peru. The only difference this time is I can buy these shoes at such a ridiculously low prices. Streets like this one are, for me, much more interesting, with loads of character and excitement, than the sterile streets of up-market areas like Miraflores. I make my way along the street, retracing the route I took in the darkness on the first night, until I am once again in the Plaza de Armas or Plaza Major. The sky is still grey which is sad when Lima is the capital of such a colourful country. I walk around admiring the colonial looking cathedral and the beautiful balconies of the Archbishop's Palace. Tomorrow I leave Peru. It is a wonderful country and if you ever get the opportunity to go, please do as Katie did and go.

I will return at a later date to explore the Amazon Basin and the jungle.

This journey took place in 2003. Many things in the travel business change on a daily bases. I know that, for example, Rail Peru have new coaches on their trains with different names and you can now reserve tickets online. It does not matter if your travel book was written one year ago or ten years ago, it is out of date before it is in print, but some things never change. Trains and hotels may alter but the magic and beauty of the locations I visited in this book are painted indelibly into the life and landscape of Peru.

Made in the USA
Middletown, DE
05 October 2018